MW01256593

HOW TO WORK

WITH

ARCHANGELS

Guidance from archangels for

abundance, healing, spiritual wisdom,

and more

Z.Z. RAE

Café House Publishing *Interlochen/Michigan*

How to work

with

Archangels

Guidance from archangels for

abundance, healing,

spiritual wisdom, and more

Z.Z. Rae

Other Books by Z.Z. Rae

Your Voice Your Choice: The Value of Every Woman

Ties of the Heart: *How to recover from Divorce and Breakups*

(A 12 step-by-step healing process)

Angel Guidance Series

Angel Guidance for Wealth *(Abundant Living for Everyone)*

Angel Guidance for Dreams *(Your Dreams explained by the Angels)*

Angel Guidance for Inner Healing *(Heal your Heart, Soul, and Mind with the Angels)*

Angel Guidance for Creativity *(Unlock your gift)*

Angel Guidance for Peace *(Lifting Life's Burdens)*

Angel Guidance for Joy *(Raise your vibrations)*

Angel Guidance for Energy Healing *(Aligning your beliefs with your desires)*

Angel Guidance for Awakening Spiritual Gifts *(Uncover your natural ability)*

Spirituality Tools

How to work with Archangels: *(Guidance from archangels for abundance, healing, spiritual wisdom, and more.)*

For my Spiritual Family and my Beautiful Angels

Note from the Author

We never worship angels, since all the glory belongs to God, but we can ask them for assistance. God gave them the task of being Heaven's helpers and messengers. Much like a spiritual UPS system, we pray to God with intention of receiving, and the angels are happy to bring us the answers.

When I think of our prayers, it reminds me of the story of Daniel, who prayed for quite some time. Suddenly, Archangel Michael showed up and explained how he'd been wrestling with a dark force, over the atmosphere, to bring Daniel his request.

Even though things may feel delayed, your angels are working their hardest to bring you what you need. Each angel has their own specialty, and when we work with them, in my own opinion, we are speeding up the process.

Just like food we eat, our environment, social influences, jobs, and how exercise will carry different energies that impact us, so does working with the positive energies of different archangels.

**Angels are a
Good Dose of
Healthy Energy
for our Daily Lives.**

I think of angels as my spiritual family who love and adore me. Whenever we need help our first impulse is to ask family or close friends. Such as: asking your dad how to fix a leaky roof, your best friend how to fix a computer, or asking your mom for a cooking lesson. That's how I see these beautiful energies. They have specialties and talents, and they can help you with what you need.

This book is a tool for you, my spiritual family, to help uplift your energy with the love from your spiritual support team. I believe each angel is a beautiful helper when we need one, but never underestimate the power of a simple prayer for help.

The more we work with angels, the more confidence we'll have in their individual energy. It is up to your personal preference to decide which angel works the best with you. Don't forget that you also have guardian angels to help you as well. I hope you enjoy your spiritual tool: *How to work with Archangels.*

-Z.Z. Rae

Chapter 1: What are Archangels?

When you think of an archangel, what pops into your head? I immediately think of a huge angel with a sword, buff, and very powerful. It also makes my mind wander to thoughts about a captain of angels or one that has a bit more authority. In the dictionary, it describes them as a chief or principal angel.

As a kid did you ever hear someone say you had a guardian angel? I remember hearing it, and I did go through an angel phase, where I was looking for them all the time. When I was probably seven-years-old, I went into our church's basement, with some other kids, and we turned off all the lights. We looked around the room trying to see an angel. Suddenly, I

looked up, and in the corner of the roor
I'm pretty sure it was a hole in the wal'
room. I proclaimed, "There's an angc

As a teen, I read a book called *This Presen..
Darkness* by Frank Peretti. In the book, he wrote about angels and how they impact our current world. It made me so much more aware. We all do have angels with us. They are our helpers to protect, love, and guide us through our life. They are divine beings of love and light, and they don't carry an agenda to boss us around with.

We have to ask for their help, since all of us have free will. When you think of the word 'angel' there is probably several things you can imagine. What the word actually means is: messenger of God. These divine beings are extensions of God to deliver messages to us. We don't worship or pray to angels, that glory belongs to our Creator, but they are like our friends, where we can ask for assistance with daily things.

When you have a bond with someone, you're not afraid to ask them for help when you feel stumped. Angels won't get mad at you for asking their help millions of times! They don't think like us.

If you get worried that you'll be dealing with a lower energy, just simply ask Jesus Christ of Nazareth or Archangel Michael to protect you, and nothing can get through to you. A protective shield will be firmly in place, and you don't need to worry.

Angels are directly connected to God Himself. These beings are pure love and light, and they don't see our failures. As I've worked with them, I noticed how they are always looking at the positive. They don't see all the junk we deal with. They never judge us where we're at, and they always lend a helping hand.

You'll never annoy the angels or archangels. They don't have egos like people. So, don't worry about asking for their help with situations. Angels aren't religious, despite what people think. They don't have a one set people they help and leave out the rest. They love every race, religion, and are eager to help everyone.

In my next upcoming book, I asked Holy Spirit about angels, and He told me that He loves when His creation helps each other. So, if you've ever thought, "Why ask angels and not God Himself?" Well, you can do both! Angels have gifts and talents just like us, and Holy Spirit loves to let them use their beautiful gifts. Unlike humans, angels don't require you to pay them back for their services. They love to help people, and you can see their hand in many ways.

When I was a teenager I lost my keys. We looked everywhere for them, and we couldn't find them. My mom asked the angels for help, with a quick prayer, and shortly after, the keys literally showed back up on the counter in plain sight!

I myself know that I have received help from angels to avoid car accidents. Just a couple years ago, I was driving on really icy roads, and I started to lose control and was about to get in a car wreck. I shouted out a prayer to Jesus, and my car and another car literally slid side-by-side together and swerved. We should've hit each other, but instead it was like a hand moved us in sync. It was crazy!

I knew the angels had protected me from harm.

When you ask the angels for help, you feel more at peace, confident, and supported. I love how when I call on them, a gentle peace comes over me in a wave. I've also felt a brush of a hand or loving words of encouragement whispered in my ears.

They are amazing!

Are you ready to meet these incredible beings of divine love and light? Let's do it!

Prayer

"Dear Father, thank you for sending your beautiful angels to help me on my life's path. Thank you for sending your protection, guidance, and healing in my life. Amen."

Chapter 2: Who is Archangel Michael?

Archangel Michael's name means:

Who is like God.

I recently started to work more and more with Archangel Michael, and I love him so much! He is such a strength when you are facing a lot of negative emotions or situations.

There are many churches named after him, and he has been sainted. Archangel Michael is located in the Bible and other sacred writings. When you think of Michael, you generally picture the typical angel—buff, sword, and powerful. Drawings of Michael depict him as having a big sword, fighting off a demon, and extremely powerful. Michael's main job is to slay fear and ego-related problems.

When I was a kid, my brother and I would play make-believe. I was always Stephanie, and he was always Michael. I find it funny how he picked that name. Michael was with me even back then, even if it was a fun game we played. When I think of the name Michael—I always feel this strength go through me, and I imagine anyone named that as strong and courageous.

Archangel Michael's Gifts
Protector

Michael is a warrior of the light, and he is the one to call on when you feel afraid or in danger. He defends with light, love, and with pure intentions. When you call on him, he will step up to help you with vehicles, your body, loved ones, your character, and belongings.

I picture Michael and Jesus working hand-in-hand. I've been calling on both of them when I feel afraid. I recently had a dream where I was driving and the vehicle went out of control, and I was headed toward some trees. I called, "Jesus, Jesus."

I soon woke up. The two accidents, I was almost in, I called on Jesus, and I was safe. So, I feel these two are partners helping us to feel secure and unafraid. Whenever you get in a vehicle, I would call on Jesus and Archangel Michael to keep you safe.

Protection of Belongings

Have you ever felt worried about something you own? Well, call on Archangel Michael to help protect your personal belongings. He's not going to feel annoyed if you ask him to keep an eye on your phone or personal device. He can be everywhere at once, so don't worry if you think it'll pull him away from more pressing matters.

Spiritual Protection

Now that I know about Archangel Michael, I call on him every time when it comes to spiritual protection. Like I said earlier, him and Jesus are pals, and I know they both keep me safe from any lower energies that may try to sneak in. Michael makes fear go packing! Call on Michael's beautiful royal purple light (that has also been described as royal blue) as a shield to keep you safe when you go about your daily life.

As an empath, or sensitive person, I often get overwhelmed by others' energies, and if you are similar, you can call on Michael's help for that. He will stand by your side and keep you covered in his purple light like a shield.

Protecting Job and Character

If you are struggling at your job or people are coming at your character, call on Archangel Michael to intervene. He can keep you safe from lower energies and people.

Life-Purpose Guidance

Do you question your life's purpose? Archangel Michael helps guide and oversee your mission on Earth. This beautiful archangel will help you with your divine calling and nudge you to the next step you should do. As of late, I have been working with Archangel Michael a lot for my life's purpose. He gives me strength when I feel low or like my work isn't impacting, and he can help you too.

Cuts Negative Ties

I've often worked with Archangel Michael to cut cords of fear from my relationships with others. He uses his sword of light to sever these cords. Not all that long ago, I was experiencing some negative emotions, and I couldn't seem to shake it. I called on Archangel

Michael to cut all fear-based ties from certain people in my life, and immediately I felt lighter.

Archangel Michael will help you feel the love in your relationships, instead of the fear-based mess we often get ourselves into.

Colors:

Gold, Royal Purple, and Royal Blue

Crystals or Gemstones:

Sugilite, Amber, Golden Topaz,

and Clear Quartz Crystal.

Scents:

Chamomile, Rosemary, Frankincense, and Sage.

Flower:

Marigold

Zodiac signs:

Sagittarius, Leo, and Aries.

Archangel Michael in a Nutshell:

- Protector
- Protection of Belongings
- Spiritual Protection
- Protecting Job and Character
- Life-Purpose Guidance
- Cuts Negative Ties

Message from Archangel Michael:

I am here to clear the air around you. When you feel weighed down, need to detox, or feel sluggish, call on me to help you with my flaming sword of love and light. You needn't be afraid when I am present around you. I am always eager to help you each day.

For some, my energy seems very strong, and you may feel a bit skittish of me when I first arrive. Do not fear, I am gentle of heart, but strong of mind. My guidance is only to help heal and restore balance within you. Be at peace.

Affirmation to Archangel Michael:

"Dear Archangel Michael, thank you for keeping me, my loved ones, my home, and all my belongings protected. Surround us with your royal purple light to keep us safe from all low energy. Guide my life's purpose and help me shine brightly."

Chapter 3: Who is Archangel Gabriel?

Archangel Gabriel's name means:

God is my strength.

When I think of angels, the one that generally pops in my mind is Gabriel. For me personally, I'd say she is the most known, although Michael comes in a close second. Of course, that could depend on who you're talking to. The story of Mary and Gabriel is extremely well known, and often I think of her as the Christmas angel.

Up until a little bit ago, I used to think of Gabriel as a he. Angels don't really have genders, but rather a certain energy. The more I've worked with her, I feel a feminine quality, and if you look at old paintings of

Gabriel, she is often painted with feminine attri
Though of course Gabriel can appear male as we
announced the birth of John the Baptist, and also is
found in the book of Daniel. Gabriel is connected to
birth, children, messengers, and creative types.

Archangel Gabriel's Gifts
Pregnancies, Raising Children, Adoptions, Births, and Conceptions.

Archangel Gabriel announced the birth of John
the Baptist and Jesus Christ, so she works well with
things related to children and pregnancies. Mother
Mary and she are a lot like Michael and Jesus—they
work well together for these causes. If you work with
children, Archangel Gabriel is the one to call by your
side to help you.

Helps with Creative Types

Gabriel is an amazing messenger, so she helps
with people who spread messages of love. Writers,
actors, teachers, artists, or counselors are just some of
the few who she works with. I myself have asked her

to help me with this book, and all my books, now that I know more about her.

Gabriel will help motivate you to get your projects done. She wants your message of love and light to spread across the world. Her skills include: opening creative doors for you and nudging you to keep walking forward.

Gabriel can give you the much-needed guidance for your creative projects. Sometimes you'll experience sparkles of copper light or flashes when working with Archangel Gabriel. Being attracted to copper can also be an indication that she is with you.

Protection Over Water/Weather

Gabriel's element is water, so she can help you with safe travels over lakes, oceans, rivers, or streams. You can also call on her concerning the weather.

Communication

Archangel Gabriel can help you with all forms of communication. If you are about to make a big speech, have a difficult discussion with someone, or want to communicate better in general, call on Gabriel. She'll give you the courage to speak up for yourself.

Colors:

Copper, Silver, White, and Pale Blue

Crystals or Gemstones:

Copper, Moonstone, Aquamarine, Pearls and Selenite.

Scents:

Jasmine, Rose, Eucalyptus and Myrrh

Flowers:

Lilies and Honesty

Zodiac Signs:

Pisces, Cancer and Scorpio.

Archangel Gabriel in a Nutshell

- Pregnancies, Raising Children, Adoptions, Births, and Conceptions.
- Helps with Creative Types
- Protection Over Water/Weather
- Communication

Message from Archangel Gabriel

I love you, dear ones, and I want to assist you in your calling within. Your desire to create is a good desire, and I wish to stir it up and bring it to its fullest height. I am here to help you through all situations concerning voicing yourself to the world. Plus, do not forget I am here to aid and assist you with children and all your needs associated with pregnancy and birth. I am here, dear ones, never fear. Never fear.

Affirmation to Archangel Gabriel

"Archangel Gabriel thank you for helping me with my creative career, communication, and any of my needs concerning pregnancy or children. Thank you for watching over my children and helping them."

Chapter 4: Who is Archangel Metatron?

Metatron means:

Either one who guards or one serves

behind [God's] throne.

Unlike the other archangels, Archangel Metatron doesn't have a name with an -el, which translates "of God". Having a little bit different of a story, Metatron and Sandalphon were both believed to have been human prophets. They lived such virtuous lives that they were given the gift of being a part of the archangel team. There isn't much information on where his name originated from. The Zohar, Talmud, and the Book of Enoch do reference Metatron as the "Lesser YHVH" (YHVH are the Hebrew letters for God). There are mentions of him sitting near God.

Some rabbis proclaim that in Exodus there is a mention of obeying an angel who is the one who brings them out of Egypt. They believe it is talking about Metatron.

Archangel Metatron's Gifts

Clears Old or Lower Energy

Archangel Metatron uses a device called the Merkabah Cube for clearing away lower energies and healing. Spinning in a clockwise manner, the cube operates on centrifugal force to drive out old energy that's no longer needed. If you need some old or lower energy cleared up, call on Metatron to help you with his healing cube.

Helps with Knowledge

Metatron is known as a scribe for God. When you need to understand more wisdom or advanced concepts, Archangel Metatron is the one to call on. He ushers in mysteries yet explained and helps adults and children to understand them.

Social Help

Archangel Metatron lends a hand to those who are highly misunderstood, sensitive, medicated, or their spiritual gifts create a social awkwardness. Call on Metatron when a child, yourself, or another needs help with working around social frustrations at work, home, or school. Although Archangel Metatron is on a higher level in the non-physical realm, he is still easily accessible, because of his once believed human nature and his enthusiasm about revealing mysteries to us all.

Helps Teach Spiritual People

Call on Metatron when you need help with learning about your spiritual gifts. He records people's choices in the Book of Life or otherwise known as the Akashic Records.

It is said that Metatron was once the great prophet Enoch from the Torah and the Bible. Since Metatron has the knowledge of life on Earth, it makes him easier to connect to.

Guards the Tree of Life

Archangel Metatron is called the angel of life. He keeps watch over the Tree of Life and is the record keeper of all that people do on Earth and in Heaven. That'd be a busy job! In the Zohar, the mystical book of Judaism, which is called the Kabbalah, it describes Archangel Metatron as "the king of angels". It says he "rules over the Tree of Knowledge of Good and Evil".

Scribe of Heaven

Metatron is described as being allowed to sit around God's throne, since he's always writing.

Angel of Children

Since in the Zohar Metatron is said to be the angel who made the way for the Children of Israel out of Egypt and helped lead them, he is known as a helper of children.

Angel of Death

Some believe that Metatron also helps those have passed to cross over.

Urges You to Change Your Thoughts

When you feel a nudge to change your negative thinking, that could be a nudge from Archangel Metatron. Since he is the keeper of the records of everything, he wants to help you with your life's purpose.

Colors:

Violet, Green, Pink Stripes, or Blue

Crystals or Gemstones:

Watermelon Tourmaline, Sardonyx (which is banded Onyx), Red or Orange Aventurine, and Mahogany Obsidian

Zodiac Sign:

Virgo

Archangel Metatron in a Nutshell

- Clears Old or Lower Energy
- Helps with Knowledge
- Social Help
- Helps Teach Spiritual People
- Guards the Tree of Life
- Scribe of Heaven (Akashic Records)
- Angel of Children
- Angel of Death
- Urges You to Change Your Thoughts

Message from Archangel Metatron

Walk wisely on Earth, and you will find great reward along the way. I am here to help you with following your inner guidance, which is connected to the divine love of who you are. I am here to clear the air! I am here to show you new discoveries within yourself and your world. There is nothing to fear. If you need aid in anything, I eagerly await your request.

Affirmation to Archangel Metatron

"Thank you, Archangel Metatron, for helping me with my spiritual career, helping clear away old energy, guiding my children, and giving me the wisdom I need for my life's purpose."

Chapter 5: Who is Archangel Uriel?

Archangel Uriel's name means:

God is my light.

Although in my past, I'd never heard of Archangel Uriel, he is normally included in the list of well-known archangels. Yet, according to some, information about him seems to contradict—unlike the other well-known archangels. He is known as the angel of transformation.

According to the Book of Enoch, Uriel went up against the Watchers, which was a collection of fallen angels, and protected the human race. He helped the prophet Enoch, who later ascended and transformed into Archangel Metatron. He generally has a flaming sword with him.

Archangel Uriel's Gifts

Gives us Information we Need

Archangel Uriel loves to give us epiphanies, ah-ha moments, ideas, information, and insights. Just like Yoda or a wise elder, Uriel is helpful for many situations.

Helps Writers, Business Issues, and Tests

If you are struggling to get ideas for your book, having trouble with business meetings, studying, or taking tests, call on Archangel Uriel. When you feel a download of thoughts and information, you'll know he's helping you.

Helps Pursuits of the Intellectual Kind

Working alongside Archangel Zadkiel, Archangel Uriel will help you do well on tests or in school to help your intellectual career.

Turns Negative into Positive

Archangel Uriel helps turn your problems into a blessing. He'll support you with challenges thrown your way.

Helps Make Clear Decisions

If you are struggling with making a choice, Archangel Uriel can help you think clearly. He aids in forgiveness, releasing old pain, and letting go of blame and anger. If you struggle with unclear thoughts, Archangel Uriel can help you with that too.

Colors:

Red and Yellow

Crystals and Gemstones:

Hematite, Obsidian, Tiger's Eye, Amber, and Rutilated Quartz

Scents:

Sandalwood, Ginger and Basil

Flowers:

Gentian and Red Hot Poker

Zodiac Sign:

Aquarius

Archangel Uriel in a Nutshell

- Gives us Information we Need

- Helps Writers, Business Issues, Tests

- Helps Pursuits of the Intellectual Kind

- Turns Negative into Positive

- Helps Make Clear Decisions

Message from Archangel Uriel

Dear, little ones, I am here to help you up from life's struggles. Contact me anytime you need help with clearing the air, connecting to higher realms, or healing from the past. I am not shy in aiding you in your daily life's struggles. Don't fret or worry about what will happen. You have an incredible team of support aiding you on this life's journey through this realm.

Affirmation to Archangel Uriel

"Dear Archangel Uriel, thank you for helping me have the information I need with my career, creativity, and life. I ask for your help to transform the negative into positive."

Chapter 6: Who is Archangel Chamuel?

Archangel Chamuel's name means:

He who sees God.

I always feel warm and fuzzy when I think of Archangel Chamuel. Although, I haven't worked with him/her a lot, I have had messages from this beautiful angel in my other books. Most consider Chamuel a he, I've felt a strong feminine energy that's very comforting.

Out of the seven archangels, which is in the 5th century Pseudo-Dionysian teachings, Chamuel is a part of the team. Apparently, people sometimes mix Samael, a dark energy who is destructive, with Chamuel. It could be the similarities of their names.

Needless to say, Chamuel is definitely an angel of light.

Located in the ancient text, the Kabbalah, Chamuel (as Kamael) is the archangel of the Geburah, the fifth Sephirah (aspect of God) on the Tree of Life. He represents courage and strength through hard times.

Kabbalists contemplate Chamuel (Kamael) as being a part of the Seraphim, which is the peak level of the heavenly angel choir. Because his name means, he who sees God, Chamuel has vision that can see everything.

Archangel Chamuel's Gifts

Self-Love

If you've been having issues of self-hatred or always putting others ahead of yourself, call on Archangel Chamuel to help you balance your self-love. This beautiful angel will help remind you that you're adored and to work on some self-love expressions.

Peace and Divine Justice

Chamuel sticks up for those who are innocent. He pours in his divine strength to help us have the power we need. He helps aid hairdressers, surgeons, air traffic controllers, animal conservationists, and anyone involved in helping keep peace.

Inner Peace

Archangel Chamuel's goal is for global peace, so he helps individuals find their inner peace for their lives when they are going through rocky times.

Missing Items

Chamuel's excellent vision helps you find items you've lost. From his high-altitude view, Chamuel spots our missing items and can clearly see the answers we are looking for with our daily problems. Even though like a great eagle, Chamuel is at a high level, he still brings himself to our Earthly realm and remains loveable and humble.

Life Purpose

Archangel Chamuel helps guide you toward your life's purpose, a more fulfilling job, a good relationship, home, or anything that you desire—as long as it's for your highest good and aligns with your higher self's purpose.

Colors:

Ruby Red or Pale Green

Crystals and Gemstones:

Red Jasper, Bloodstone, Fluorite, Carnelian, and Pink Tourmaline.

Scents:

Mint, Geranium, Neroli, and Ginger.

Zodiac Sign:

Taurus

Archangel Chamuel in a Nutshell

- Self-love
- Peace and Divine Justice
- Inner Peace
- Missing Items
- Life's purpose, relationships, jobs

Message from Archangel Chamuel

I'm here to heighten your awareness of who you truly are. I'm here to pour out loving energy into your heart, soul, and mind to help aid the world in abundance of love, peace, and joy. I'm here to provide a path for you, when it seems the path is full of fear. Take my hand, little ones, and I'll guide you around the pitfalls that pop up along the way.

You have a divine purpose, and sometimes it can feel cloudy to see the truest and best path. I'm here to take a fan and blow away all the confusion you've felt in the past. Don't fret about tomorrow, for I'm with you to help you deal with each day. Forgive daily, and let love flood you concerning your relationships, jobs, and all your accomplishments. You are very beautiful, little ones, and I want to show you that inner beauty always.

Affirmation to Archangel Chamuel

"Dear Archangel Chamuel, thank you for helping me find things that I'm looking for. I gladly ask for help from you concerning my life's purpose, and I thank you for helping me uncover it every day."

Chapter 7: Who is Archangel Ariel?

Archangel Ariel's name means:

Lion of God.

Archangel Ariel is the nature angel. She's mentioned in Coptic, apocryphal, and mystical Judeo-Christian writings. In these writings, she's also said to be a manager of the underworld. In the play, The Tempest, Shakespeare spoke of how Ariel was a tree sprite.

Archangel Ariel's Gifts

Healing

Ariel and Archangel Raphael work hand and hand when it comes to healing. Ariel's specialty is healing animals. She will give you her loving help if one of your animals are ill or if you find an injured animal in nature.

Watches Over Nature

Archangel Ariel is said to be an overseer of the angel choir who keep the order of the universe in balance—such as the sun, stars, moon, and planets.

Helps Those in Environmental Fields

If you feel a tug to work in helping heal the planet, Archangel Ariel is the one to help you with this mission.

Watches over Earth

Ariel helps keep watch over the natural resources of our planet. She helps make sure animals and people are treated well.

Our Daily Needs

Since Archangel Ariel helps keep watch over all nature's resources, she can help you with your daily needs as well. She takes care that people have enough healthy food, shelter, and clean water.

Safety in Nature

Archangel Ariel takes your hand and aids you with working with nature safely. If you love camping or hiking, call upon Ariel to watch over you as you go.

Connects You to the Non-physical Side of Nature

If you want to be able to connect with the non-physical side of nature, Archangel Ariel will gladly help reveal it to you. Ariel will usher you into the world of fairies, elementals, or other sides of nature you can't see with your physical eyes.

Keeping Ariel at your side will open your awareness of the spirits of nature who live in flowers, trees, gardens, lakes and streams.

Color:

Pale Pink

Crystals or Gemstones:

Rose Quartz, Apatite, Agate (especially Moss and Tree agates), and Jasper (such as the Leopardskin and Dalmatian varieties)

Zodiac Sign:

Aries

Archangel Ariel in a Nutshell

- Healing
- Watches Over Nature
- Helps Those in Environmental Fields
- Watches Over Earth
- Our Daily Needs
- Safety in Nature

- Connects you to Non-physical Side of Nature

Message from Archangel Ariel

Treat others with kindness each day. Spreading kindness will open your heart to great abilities and bigger capacities than ever before. When you treat a child, animal, or a person with respect, love, and care, that same respect and care will manifest in your life. Take care of your environment, loved ones, because it is all you have in this physical realm.

If you treat your environment poorly, there is consequences to it. Not to frighten you with negativity, but your world needs your help, little ones. Take care of the little beasts who roam around you; for they too are a part of your daily world. Take care of yourself; for you also are a valuable asset to this world. Do you feel led to clean up the world around you? Take care to call on me if you feel you do not know where to start by loving your planet. I will show you a beautiful path available for you.

Affirmation to Archangel Ariel

"Thank you, Archangel Ariel for helping me connect with nature and treat it kindly. Open my eyes to the non-physical realm of nature and help me be a vessel to bring healing."

Chapter 8: Who is Archangel Sandalphon?

Archangel Sandalphon's name means:

Brother.

Archangel Sandalphon's origin is much like Archangel Metatron. He was said to be the Biblical prophet Elijah, who went up into heaven on a chariot of fire. Working almost in sync, Metatron watches over the exit of the Tree of Life, where Sandalphon is the guard over the entrance to the spheres of the Tree of Life.

Archangel Sandalphon's Gifts

Helps Bring Prayers to God

One of the gifts of Archangel Sandalphon is being the go-between from people to God. He helps deliver prayers. This function could be because Sandalphon is described as a very tall angel—reaching Heaven to Earth.

Helps Determine a Child's Gender

Sandalphon is said to help determine a child's gender.

Aids Musicians, Writers, and Those Who Help with Unborn Children

If you are a musician, you can gain help by calling on Sandalphon to assist you. When you're learning a new song, or trying to learn an instrument, ask Sandalphon for help. Plus, he also helps writers, midwives, and people aiding with childbirth.

Support for Your Spirituality

Another role Sandalphon plays is connecting you to God and your divine nature. His kind and gentle presence can help you feel more deeply in tune with your spirituality and God. You'll be flooded with love and the emotion of feeling cared for and watched over.

Oversees Prosperity, Strength, and Beauty

Call upon Sandalphon if you need help with prosperity, spiritual strength, or openness and awareness of the beauty of life.

Unborn Children

Sandalphon is given the mission of taking care of unborn children, and you can ask him to assist you with any problems with fertility, pregnancy, and birth.

Releases Emotional Blocks

When you are struggling with emotions such as: guilt, fear, emotional blocks, or aggressiveness, call on Archangel Sandalphon to help you overcome these things.

Color:

Turquoise

Crystals or Gemstones:

Turquoise and Calcite (any variety)

Zodiac Sign:

Pisces

Archangel Sandalphon in a Nutshell

- Helps Bring Prayers to God
- Helps Determine a Child's Gender
- Aids Musicians, Writers, and Those Who Help with Unborn Children
- Support for Your Spirituality

- Oversees Prosperity, Strength, and Beauty
- Unborn Children
- Releases Emotional Blocks

Message from Archangel Sandalphon

Clear away all the fear, dear ones, you don't need that anymore. If you would like help with your higher wisdom, I am here for your assistance. I can see you for who you truly are, and you don't need to worry about how your life will unfold. Each day is beautiful, and I can help you with the wisdom you are seeking for your spiritual career and path. Don't worry about the how and the whys of life, it'll work in your favor if you so believe and ask. Don't fear for your little children, for they are watched over by me and the Father.

Affirmation to Archangel Sandalphon

"Dear Archangel Sandalphon, thank you for helping me with my spirituality and my higher calling. I ask for your help with my music and writing."

Chapter 9: Who is Archangel Zadkiel?

Archangel Zadkiel's name means:

Righteousness of God.

Archangel Zadkiel (sometimes known as Tzadkiel, Zachiel or Zedkiel), is the angel to call on when you need a comforting touch, abundance, or healing. Zadkiel is known as the gentlest of all the archangels.

When you look into Jewish writings, Zadkiel is the archangel who brings out compassion and forgiveness within ourselves and others. Zadkiel (as Tzadkiel) governs over the fourth, or Chesed, Sephirah on the Tree of Life in the Kabbalah.

The Chesed sphere helps in aiding one to work on unending love and kindness and expressing it on the Earth. Zadkiel is known as one of the seven archangels in the Gnostic beliefs and also in the Pseudo-Dionysius texts. Having the name Zachariel, Zadkiel is recognized as one of the seven cherished archangels by Pope Saint Gregory.

Archangel Zadkiel's Gifts

Angel of Memory

Archangel Zadkiel can help you when you are struggling to remember figures and facts, especially if you are a student.

Healing Painful Memories

If you are struggling to recover from a rough past, call on Archangel Zadkiel for healing. He can spark the remembrance of your true nature and help you walk in forgiveness. If you struggle with feeling like a victim, Zadkiel can help you walk out of that emotion and into a powerful new mindset.

Emotional Healing

When calling on Zadkiel for emotional health, he'll help you refocus from the pain and back toward the joyful moments you have in your life.

Healer of the Mind

If your mental health is rocky, Zadkiel can gently bring you healing. He'll remind you that you are the one who is responsible for your own source of happiness. If you struggle with depression or different emotional needs, Zadkiel is the one to ask for help. With a dagger, which emanates violet or blue light, Zadkiel will help you cut through those dark cords.

Helps Children

If a child is in need, Zadkiel is eager to help them overcome their problems.

Abundance

If you are struggling in the area of abundance, whether it's in a material way or spiritual way, Zadkiel is a great helper.

Guide for Unique Careers

If you are thinking of going into a unique career such as a Reiki master, aromatherapist, librarian, interpreter, or psychiatrist, call on Zadkiel to help.

Colors:

Sky Blue, Violet, and Deep Indigo Blue

Crystals and Gemstones

Blue Lace Agate, Amethyst, Blue Chalcedony, and Lapis Lazuli

Scents:

Sandalwood, Ylang Ylang, Bergamot, Rosemary, and Nutmeg

Flower:

Violet

Zodiac Sign:

Gemini

Archangel Zadkiel in a Nutshell

- Angel of Memory

- Healing Painful Memories
- Emotional Healing
- Healer of the Mind
- Helps Children
- Abundance
- Guide for Unique Careers

Message from Archangel Zadkiel

Treasure the moments you have now; for they are very precious and unique. Don't fret so much about the past and all its fears and worries; for you are not living in that experience anymore.

Lift your face upward and expect the very best out of each moment you have. Do away with worry; it doesn't serve you anyways. Let go of the fears of the past. They don't serve you either. I am here to help you walk through things and help you let it go. Fear not, little ones, you are watched over by us.

Affirmation to Archangel Zadkiel

"Dear Archangel Zadkiel, thank you for guiding me through my inner healing, helping me find the things I need, and aiding with abundance."

Chapter 10: Who is Archangel Raguel?

Archangel Raguel's name means:

Friend of God.

Archangel Raguel is primarily written about in the apocryphal Book of Enoch and is recorded as one of the seven principal archangels.

Archangel Raguel's Gifts

Orderliness, Harmony, Fairness, and Justice

In the book of Enoch, Raguel brought about justice to those who went up against God's will. He also governs the affairs between humans and angels.

Heals Arguments

When you're facing a disagreement or conflict involving misunderstandings, Raguel is an angel to call on for help.

Attracts Friendships

In order to usher in some balanced situations and beautiful new friendships, call on Archangel Raguel. Because Raguel's name means "friend of God" he helps turn turbulent relationships into harmony.

Angel Over Snow and Ice

Raguel carries around a glorious flaming sword, which can be used to melt ice or snow.

Relationship with Yourself

Archangel Raguel can help you not only with your friendships, but the relationship you have with yourself. If you struggle with loving yourself, call on Raguel to help heal that relationship as well.

Colors:

Dark/Pale Blue

Crystals and Gemstones:

Milky Quartz, Moonstone, and Aquamarine

Zodiac Sign:

Sagittarius

Archangel Raguel in a Nutshell

- Orderliness, Harmony, Fairness, and Justice.
- Heals Arguments
- Attracts Friendships
- Angel Over Snow and Ice
- Relationship with Yourself

Message from Archangel Raguel

In order to bring harmony to your relationships, you must first balance the relationship with your sense of self. Open your heart up to healing and love, and you will find your other relationships being filled with peace and love as well. In order to connect to divine peace and love, simply see a beautiful harmonious light filling your entire being and flowing from your heart to others.

Affirmation to Archangel Raguel

"Dear Archangel Raguel, thank you for bringing peace in all my relationships and helping me attract the right friends in my life. I choose to be at harmony with myself, and I thank you for helping me."

Chapter 11: Who is Archangel Raziel?

Archangel Raziel's name means:

Secret of God.

Archangel Raziel (known as Ratziel) is the archangel that is over the Chokmah, the second Sephirah (an aspect of God) of the Tree of Life, found in the Kabbalah. Raziel takes our own natural wisdom and turns it into a higher spiritual wisdom. We then can put that wisdom into practice in a meaningful way. To keep us attentive and to avoid distractions, the Chokmah sphere is used. In order to use the sphere, we have to tune into our higher self which is linked to divine wisdom. Often Raziel's energy is similar to an ancient wizard like Merlin but with massive eagle wings.

Archangel Raziel's Gifts

Wisdom

Raziel loves to give you mysterious wisdom, especially when it comes with the purpose of healing. He helps with the practicality of using that wisdom in our daily lives.

Spiritual Practices

If you are desiring how to learn more about your spiritual gift, such as psychic abilities, discovering the roots of illnesses, dream interpretation, and being able to use your resources in a wise manner, Raziel will aid you.

Support for Career

Raziel is a supporter of scientists, astrologers, secret service, and clairvoyants.

Life's Mission

Your soul goes through many lessons, and Raziel helps pull in all the pieces and shows you how to use it for your life's mission.

Heals Trauma from the Past

If you've suffered from a lot of trauma and memories that resurface, Raziel guides you into healing. He helps you deal with your fears and nudges you toward the right steps concerning your life's purpose here on Earth.

Dissolves Past Vows

Life vows from the past can muddy up our here and now. Raziel helps get rid of those commitments such as: vows of self-sacrifice, poverty, or chastity. If you need those vows broken, call upon Raziel to help you.

Colors:

Rainbow Colors

Crystals and Gemstones:

Peridot, Apache Tears, Clear Quartz, and Aqua Aura Crystals

Archangel Raziel in a Nutshell

- Wisdom
- Spiritual Practices
- Support for Career
- Life's Mission
- Heals Trauma from the Past
- Dissolves Past Vows

Message from Archangel Raziel

Greater wisdom is inside each and every one of you. All you need to do is tune into the right frequency, and BAM, you'll have an instant download of the answers you are seeking in your current life. If you need a boost, a pick-me-up, or a gentle nudge, call on me to help you with your life's purpose.

I see the calling on each of you, and each of you have a beautiful reason for being here. Perhaps you can tune into the energy I am releasing. When you do, you'll find it much easier to access that deep founded wisdom you are searching for. There are teachers, messages, and many things I am sending your way to depict what you need to do. Follow your gut, and see where the deep wisdom flows.

Affirmation to Archangel Raziel

"Dear Archangel Raziel, thank you for helping me with my life's purpose. I love how your wisdom is easy to understand, and I can put it into practical use. I allow healing to flow through my body, and I know you help me with healing my past."

Chapter 12: Who is Archangel Haniel?

Archangel Haniel's name means:

Glory of God.

Archangel Haniel keeps watch over the seventh, or Netzach, Sephirah (emanation of God's will) in the Kabbalah. This portion of the Sefirot characterizes overcoming our inside world, imagination, emotions, and intuition. Humans' natural free will is marked by the Netzach Sephirah, and also represents resolve and stamina. It's the full expression of love here on Earth.

Archangel Haniel's Gifts

Higher Vision

Are you drawn to clairvoyance? Archangel Haniel can aid you in practicing your seeing abilities and intuition or other forms of revered feminine energy.

Full Moon Releasing

When the full moon is up, Haniel can be of assistance to help you heal and rid yourself of any old toxic emotions. If you are dealing with womanly issues, Haniel can help with that too.

Spiritual Gifts

When you're learning to tap into your spiritual gifts, Haniel is a guidance into your inner world. Even though there is feminine energy coming from Haniel, men also can reap benefits from a connection to her— since men carry this type of energy as well. Just as men have feminine energy, women have male energy. Haniel brings awakening to inner wisdom and guidance for all.

Artists and Marriage

If you need help as an artist or in matters such as marriage or children, Haniel will assist you with your needs.

Color:

Pale Blue (Moonlight)

Crystals and Gemstones:

Rose Quartz, Pink Calcite, Chrysoprase, and Moonstone

Zodiac Sign:

Oversees all

Archangel Haniel in a Nutshell

- Higher Vision
- Full Moon Releasing
- Spiritual Gifts
- Artists and Marriage

Message from Archangel Haniel

Beautiful things are happening inside of you, little ones. I can see each thing like a precious, little bud about to bloom. Take heart that things are in motion for you in the right season and time. I will help open your eyes to see beyond your natural abilities. Trust what you are sensing, feeling, seeing, hearing, tasting, smelling, and touching. You have great insight buried inside of you. Use your God-given talents to bring light into the world and further the cause of love and light.

Affirmation to Archangel Haniel

"Dear Archangel Haniel, thank you for awakening my intuition and helping me clearly see what I need to see. I release all past issues, and I thank you for helping me clear them."

Chapter 13: Who is Archangel Jophiel?

Archangel Jophiel's name means:

Beauty of God.

GERVBIM   IOPHIEL

Vindicibus gladijs expellimus omne profanum   Crisp. de Pas
vendtor   es templo quin et Adame fuge   inu. exc.

Archangel Jophiel, (sometimes written as Iophiel or Zaphiel) shows up as one of the seven archangels in Pseudo-Dionysius's De Coelesti

Hierarchia ("Celestial Hierarchy"). This is a 5th-century text on angelology which has been significant in Christian theology. She is recognized as the angel of illumination and creative power.

It's known that this theology impacted Thomas Aquinas's writings as he talked about the nine choirs of angels. Jophiel sometimes makes an appearance as being extremely tall (over 9 feet), wearing a yellow cloak, and wielding a flaming sword.

In Jewish tradition, Archangel Jophiel was the first mentioned angel. She was the one who drove Adam and Eve out of the Garden of Eden with her flaming sword. Because she had the honor of doing so, she is left to guard the Tree of Life.

Archangel Jophiel's Gifts

Since Archangel Jophiel means, "beauty of God" she has a feminine energy that uplifts situations and brings the beauty out of them. Here are some things she beautifies.

Loving Feelings

If you ask her, Jophiel will flood your heart and body with good feelings of love and gratitude. If you feel a gentle touch on your brow and a loving embrace, that's Jophiel reminding you of all the good in your life.

Home and Office

Decluttering your work space can help uplift your thoughts and energy, so that you can relax. If you feel a nudge to declutter, that could be Jophiel trying to help beautify your environment.

Beautifying Thoughts

When facing negative thoughts, Archangel Jophiel can help you see the beauty in your relationships, life, and the situations you face. She will breathe beauty over your mind to help uplift you each day.

Self-love

If you struggle in the department of self-love or self-care, call on Jophiel to help you beautify your mindset toward yourself. She can help you with feeling better about your appearance and who you are.

Learning New Things

Jophiel loves to lend a helping hand when you are tackling a new thing. When it comes to spiritual matters, she loves to help show you your own potential.

Inspiration

If you're having trouble with inspiration, call on Jophiel to help untangle your thought process. She'll reveal to you your untapped potential you have inside.

Environment

Environmental issues are something Jophiel is passionate about. If you wish to help in that area, call on Jophiel to assist you.

Negative to Positive

Struggling with negative thoughts can be difficult. Call on Archangel Jophiel if you need help transforming your thoughts from negative to positive. If you are having a hard time in a relationship, you can call on her to help clear up the misunderstanding.

Beauty

Jophiel helps in a lot of areas including assistance with your appearance such as: wardrobe, makeup, and hair.

Helps Clean Out the Old

When you get a sudden urge to start donating or selling items that you no longer need, it's more and likely Archangel Jophiel. She understands how our environment can impact us, so she may start nudging you to clean up the area around you.

Color:

Dark Pink

Crystals or Gemstones:

Rubellite, Deep Pink Tourmaline, Ametrine, Smokey Quartz, and Rutilated Quartz

Scents:

Lavender, Orange, Myrrh, and Lemongrass

Zodiac Sign:

Libra

Archangel Jophiel in a Nutshell

- Loving Feelings
- Home and Office
- Beautifying Thoughts
- Self-love
- Learning New Things
- Inspiration
- Environment
- Negative to Positive
- Beauty
- Helps Clean Out the Old

Message from Archangel Jophiel

Let go of that which no longer serves you. You don't need things that are heavy that drag you down. If you look around your environment and see items that no longer serve you, purge those things, and lovingly let them go. There are times when possessions serve you, and then later on they no longer have a loving purpose for you.

When those items no longer add to your life, it's time to release and surrender those things. The energy of your environment is impacted by those items you hold onto—whether you think they do or not. Things can impact your energy or mood on a daily basis. If you struggle with your thoughts of a negative nature, simply turn toward the things that please you.

What subjects are uplifting? What makes you feel good? Do you feel good when you look at a picture on your wall? Do you feel good when you look at your child? Think on those things—instead of the dragging subjects that hold you down. Uplift your energy, darlings.

Affirmation to Archangel Jophiel

"Dear Archangel Jophiel, thank you for helping me purge out what I no longer need in my life. I ask for help to keep my thoughts healthy and happy."

Chapter 14: Who is Archangel Raphael?

Archangel Raphael's name means:

God heals; God's healer.

With an aura of green light, Archangel Raphael is long known as the angel of healing. I always picture him and Jesus working side by side to bring health to me. Even though Raphael isn't mentioned in the Bible, he is said to be the archangel who stirred the pool of Bethesda, which is mentioned in the Gospels.

Another story where Raphael is thought to be mentioned is when the three angels visited Abraham and his wife. He is also said to be the angel who healed Jacob, after he wrestled with the Angel of the Lord, and the one who gave King Solomon his magical ring.

In the book of Tobit, Raphael hears the prayers of Tobit and Sarah. He aids Tobit's son, Tobias, on his journey to bring healing to both. Sarah, inflicted by a demon, has had seven husbands die whenever she marries. Tobit, a righteous man, goes blind and prays for death. On the journey, Raphael instructs Tobias how to deliver Sarah and drive out the demon. He also gives the cure for his father's blindness. The story is beautiful and shows the mercy and healing of God.

Archangel Raphael's Gifts

Safe Travels

Since the story of Tobias, Raphael is well known as the angel of healing and helping travelers get to where they need to go. If you are traveling and need protection, call on Raphael to help you.

New Business Avenues

If a new idea for a business is brewing in your mind, call on Raphael to help you with the steps you need to take. Buying, selling, writing, or business—Raphael can help you with each of them.

Helps Children

When your child is sick or needs help, call on Raphael to aid you. He loves children and will eagerly help.

Memory

When your memory seems to be fading, call on Raphael to help you improve it. He also can be of assistance when you are learning a brand-new language.

Knowledge and Healing

Archangel Raphael is known as the angel of healing and knowledge. He is often depicted as having a staff and a medicine jar. Many times, instant healing happens when you ask Raphael for his healing touch on your body.

There has been accounts where people feel a gentle buzzing energy when Raphael is working on them. Or others have seen green lights. Raphael's healing may also come about in a slower way, helping ease short term or long-term pain. Asking for help is key.

Clears Away Fear and Stress

Archangel Raphael and Michael both work hand in hand to dissolve stress and fear, especially when those things are impacting your health. When you lean on Raphael and get to know him, the more you'll be able to trust his healing, gentle work on you.

Emotional Healing

Raphael can also work on emotional healing. When emotional healing transpires, it tends to bring about a physical healing in the body as well.

Helps to Find the Right Healer

Sometimes Raphael will lead you to find the right doctor, counselor, dentist, therapist, or other specialized healer. Raphael may also nudge you to start eating a healthier diet.

Colors:

Emerald Green and Yellow

Crystals or Gemstones:

Emerald, Malachite, Citrine, Aventurine, and Yellow Calcite

Scents:

Lavender, Lily of the Valley, Mint, Bergamot, and Thyme

Flower:

Iris

Zodiac Sign:

Oversees All

Archangel Raphael in a Nutshell

- Safe Travels
- New Business Avenues
- Helps Children
- Memory

- Knowledge and Healing
- Clears Away Fear and Stress
- Emotional Healing
- Helps to Find the Right Healer

Message from Archangel Raphael

Guidance lies within you, and it's up to you to follow it concerning your life. I am here to help aid you with what you need. If you feel a nudge to do this or that, trust that guidance, for it is your angels helping you understand your own inner wisdom.

We are here to help train you in what you need to do to be successful in your life. Many things may feel like they pull you back and forth, but if you reach out for help, you'll find everything you need to move forward. If you are desiring good health and guidance, I am here to assist you daily.

Affirmation to Archangel Raphael

"Dear Archangel Raphael, thank you for helping me stay healthy and strong. I'm thankful for your aid concerning my life, my own guidance, my inner healing, and the path of health for my life."

Chapter 15: Who is Archangel Jeremiel?

Archangel Jeremiel means:

God uplifts.

Archangel Jeremiel makes his appearance in Eastern Orthodox tradition and in a few noncanonical and Coptic books such as 2 Esdras.

In 2 Esdras, it shows discussions between Ezra and Jeremiel. Jeremiel talks about how he keeps an eye over the passed-on souls from the great flood. Jeremiel is named among the seven archangels in the Ethiopian Book of Enoch—and is known as Ramiel. In 2 Baruch, the non-canonical text, Jeremiel (Ramiel) is said to be the angel who brings hope and helps the souls who are going to Heaven. He awakens spiritual clairvoyance and visions and can help you take a look at your life.

Archangel Jeremiel's Gifts

Helps Those Who are Crossing Over

Archangel Jeremiel takes the hands of those who've departed, helps them take stock of their lives, and ushers them to Heaven.

Take Stock of Life

If you need help with adjusting things in your life, Jeremiel can help with that. He's not just an angel to usher the departed to the other side, but also helps you refocus to remember your life's purpose.

Mentor

Archangel Jeremiel is a teacher and mentor who helps us to look at ourselves with love.

Color:

Dark Purple

Crystal or Gemstone:

Amethyst

Archangel Jeremiel in a Nutshell

- Helps Those Who are Crossing Over

- Take Stock of Life

- Mentor

Message from Archangel Jeremiel

Take heed of your life each day, and don't worry so much. How you invest now will impact your future plans as well. Yet don't worry about all the little things so much. I am here to help you with those little choices you are confused about. There is great success waiting for you, and each day you invest is another day closer to that beautiful success you seek.

Affirmation to Archangel Jeremiel

"Dear Archangel Jeremiel, thank you for your inner guidance. Open my spiritual eyes, so I can clearly see the path I should take for my life."

Chapter 16: Who is Jesus?

The name Jesus means:

Rescue, Deliver.

Although not an archangel, I wanted to touch on Jesus, since I work so well with Him. I believe Jesus' energy is powerful, and if you are close-knit with Him, He will forever help your life. My personal belief is that He is the Son of God, though if you believe otherwise that is okay too—He will still work with you to help you.

Jesus Christ, or Jesus of Nazareth, was a radical Jew who became the cornerstone of Christianity. Fulfilling prophesy, Jesus was the written about awaited Messiah that was testified in the Old Testament. Almost all scholars proclaim Jesus existed throughout history, though they don't all agree on the historical Jesus verses the Biblical Jesus.

Jesus taught life-changing messages, healed the sick, told parables, and was crucified by Pontius Pilate. Later on, Jesus was risen from the dead and ascended into Heaven.

Jesus' Gifts

Protection

I could tell a million stories from people I know about how Jesus has protected them. For me personally, I remember on two different occasions calling on Jesus, and I was saved from being in a car accident. He is an amazing protector, and I think of Him and Michael as the bouncers of Heaven. If you ever feel scared or a lower energy is around, call on Jesus, He'll get that thing running.

Healing

Jesus was moved with compassion and healed the sick. There are countless stories in the Bible of His miracles. I also have seen people healed by calling on Him. When I was a teenager, one of my friends was believing for Jesus to heal her foot. She couldn't even touch it to the ground without shooting pains going through it. One Sunday night we were having intense worship. I was singing a song, and the words were saying, "Jump, jump, jump in the new wine."

As I spoke the words, "jump, jump, jump", I knew that my friend needed to jump, and she'd be healed. I got off the piano, and I started madly twirling. I've never twirled like this before. In fact, I'd probably puke if I tried to do what I did that day. After I twirled like crazy, I went over to her, along with a few other girls, and we grabbed her hands and started to jump.

As she jumped her foot was instantly healed!

Another time, I remember feeling like I wanted to puke. I laid on the couch and over and over I said, "By the stripes of Jesus I am healed." I wouldn't quit.

After just a little while, the nausea completely left, and I was totally healed. I could go on and on!

A lady at our church had been in a surgery, and the doctors had left an instrument inside her. She didn't want more surgery, so she asked for prayer. She came up front, and we laid hands on her in Jesus' name. Instantly she started to bend and shout for joy. When she went back to the doctor, she discovered that the instrument was completely gone!

My mom had been experiencing ringing in her ears for months and months. She was telling me about it, so I laid my hands on her and prayed in Jesus' name, and instantly the ringing stopped. Another time, she was going through bad back pain, and again I did the same thing, and her pain instantly left. Jesus is an incredible healer.

Life Messages

Jesus was a powerful teacher, and He used illustrations to move crowds. He also helps us today with His teaching, and if you ask Him for life messages and help, He will give them to you. He is a great mentor to help you with your life's purpose and plan.

Emotional Healing

Jesus loved the adulterer, the prostitute, and the leper. He loves to help heal emotional wounds in people. He's non-judgmental. There have been several times in my own life where He pulled me through an emotional battle.

When I was going through my divorce, a wonderful prayer counselor named Nathan Blouse, who runs The Safe Place, used a beautiful prayer method with Jesus. When I went into the prayer session, memories popped up, and with the help of Nathan Blouse and Jesus, I released the memories and healed them.

Jesus steps in and shows love in the midst of the worst trauma and can help you gently love, accept, and approve of yourself. He will show you the path of healing in the most loving way possible. If you want more information about The Safe Place check out www.inthesafeplace.com

Friendship

Jesus is a brother figure, and He is kind-hearted toward anyone who wants a friend. He is the friend that truly will stick closer than a brother. If you feel lonely, call on Jesus to help you through the feelings you're facing. He can help bring the right friends into your life.

Comforter

Whenever I think of Jesus, I think of a comforting shepherd who picks up a wounded lamb. He is gentle of heart and will help you up when you are down.

One time I was completely a mess, and I kept hearing Jesus say, "I am with you. I'm never going to leave you. I'm here." As He continued to speak, I felt more and more peace come over me.

Loves Children

Jesus loves kids, and if you are struggling with your children, call on Him to help guide you. In the scriptures, the little children climbed all over Him, and His disciples rebuked them. Instead of agreeing, Jesus said, "Let the little children come to me, and do not hinder them, for the kingdom of heaven belongs to such as these."

When I was little, I constantly sang songs to Jesus. I knew he was my friend, and I loved that He was always by my side.

Spiritual Gifts

I believe Jesus had all the spiritual gifts, so if you need a mentor, call on Him to help you develop your spiritual abilities. He had unique qualities such as perceiving thoughts, walking on water, multiplying bread, and raising the dead. Jesus wants us to operate in the gifts like He did.

As a teen, Jesus helped me develop my intuitive gifts. I'd start getting messages, and slowly I began to trust what I felt as I grew in my relationship with Him. I've experienced clairvoyance (visions), a powerful presence of Jesus, clairaudient (hearing) experiences, clairsentient (feelings), and audible voices from two angels.

The more I've learned to trust what I'm getting, the stronger it has become in my life. We all have our individual spiritual journeys, so even if you don't believe the same as me, it's okay. But, I know Jesus is eager to help anyone who asks.

Colors:

All the Colors

Flower:

Lilly of the Valley (at least I think of this flower when I think of Jesus raising from the dead.)

Signs:

For a while, in church, I would get glitter on my hands after I was done with worship. I called it my "Jesus sparkles". I have also heard of people seeing oil, finding gemstones, or smelling sweet smells—all of which is associated with Jesus.

Jesus in a Nutshell

- Protection
- Healing
- Life Messages
- Emotional Healing
- Friendship
- Comforter

- Loves Children
- Spiritual Gifts

Message from Jesus

You are my beautiful children, and I love you unconditionally. If you need anything just ask Me, and I will gladly give it to you. I will help lead you in the direction you need to go, so never fear. I am with you always, so if you need a hand to hold, please reach out to me and know I am with you always. I love you.

Prayer to Jesus

"Dear Jesus, thank you for always being with me. I am grateful for your help with my daily life. Thank you for healing my body, helping me with my purpose, and walking with me every day. Amen."

Chapter 17: Who is Mother Mary?

The name Mary means:

Wished-for child; rebellion; bitter.

When I think of Mother Mary, I think of a gentle heart—a nurturer. In the Gospels, Mary is visited by Archangel Gabriel who announced that she would be with child by the Holy Spirit.

After she passed, it was said her body was directly brought to Heaven. Over centuries, many believers have told stories how Mother Mary has visited them.

Mother Mary's Gifts

Nurtures and Guides

Known as the Mother of God, Mother Mary is a beautiful energy who nurtures and guides. She helps people develop their Christ-like nature, so that we can grow in our spiritual light toward ourselves and others.

Healing, Music, Truth

Archangel Raphael and Mother Mary work together to help aid with wholeness, healing, music, truth, clarity, and invention.

Love

Mother Mary is a divine love and nurturing energy. She shows us acceptance, compassion, and unconditional love. She soothes, uplifts, and helps those who call on her to feel peaceful, safe, and loved.

Protector

Known as the Star of the Sea, Mother Mary helps keep fisherman, sailors, and those living near the water safe.

Queen of Angels

Mother Mary is called the Queen of Angels, which seems rather fitting since she birthed the King of Heaven.

Helps Troubled Souls

When struggling with troublesome worries, Mother Mary reassures a fearful heart. She helps soothe and heal the pain you've faced.

Helps Connect Us to the Divine

Some people have a hard time connecting to the Divine, so Mother Mary takes their hand and helps them with their link. She helps heal those who are downcast or wounded and gives them healing, guidance, support, and shows them their inner light.

Self-love

Mother Mary carries a powerful feminine energy and helps us work on our self-love. She is full of compassion, protection, and unconditional love.

Illumination

Mother Mary is connected to the Divine, so she sees what is, what will be, and has a broader view. She can bring about illumination if you ask her.

Color:

Baby Blue

Crystal or Gemstone:

Rhodochrosite

Scent:

Rose

Flower:

Rose

Mother Mary in a Nutshell

- Nurtures and Guides

- Healing, Music, Truth

- Love

- Protector

- Queen of Angels

- Helps Troubled Souls

- Helps Connect Us to the Divine

- Self-love

- Illumination

Message from Mother Mary

All I have is love for you, little ones—endless love. If you are lacking in feeling love over yourself or others, call on me to help illuminate your connection to the Divine. I have resources available for you, if you but ask of me. I am not ever withholding connection, love, and peace—it is always available for you.

Affirmation to Mother Mary

"Dear Mother Mary, thank you for helping me be nurturing, have compassion, and love toward myself and others. I thank you for illumination and growth inside of me."

Quick Angel Reference

Archangel Michael

- Protector
- Protection of Belongings
- Spiritual Protection
- Protecting Job and Character
- Life-Purpose Guidance
- Cuts Negative Ties

Archangel Gabriel

- Pregnancies, Raising Children, Adoptions, Births, and Conceptions.
- Helps with Creative Types
- Protection over Water/Weather
- Communication

Archangel Metatron

- Clears Old or Lower Energy
- Helps with Knowledge
- Social Help
- Helps Teach Spiritual People
- Guards the Tree of Life
- Scribe of Heaven (Akashic Records)

- Angel of Children
- Angel of Death
- Urges You to Change Your Thoughts

Archangel Uriel

- Gives Us Information We Need

- Helps Writers, Business Issues, Tests

- Helps Pursuits of the Intellectual Kind

- Turns Negative into Positive

- Helps Make Clear Decisions

Archangel Chamuel

- Self-love
- Peace and Divine Justice
- Inner Peace
- Missing Items
- Life's Purpose, Relationships, Jobs

Archangel Ariel

- Healing
- Watches Over Nature
- Helps Those in Environmental Fields
- Watches Over Earth

- Our Daily Needs
- Safety in Nature
- Connects You to Non-physical Side of Nature

Archangel Sandalphon

• Helps Bring Prayers to God

• Helps Determine a Child's Gender

• Aids Musicians, Writers, and Those Who Help with Unborn Children

• Support for Your Spirituality

• Oversees Prosperity, Strength, and Beauty

• Unborn Children

• Releases Emotional Blocks

Archangel Zadkiel

• Angel of Memory

• Healing Painful Memories

• Emotional Healing

• Healer of the Mind

- Helps Children

- Abundance

- Guide for Unique Careers

Archangel Raguel

- Orderliness, Harmony, Fairness, and Justice.

- Heals Arguments

- Attracts Friendships

- Angel Over Snow and Ice

- Relationship with Yourself

Archangel Raziel

- Wisdom

- Spiritual Practices

- Support for Career

- Life's Mission

- Heals Trauma from the Past

- Dissolves Past Vows

Archangel Haniel

- Higher Vision

- Full Moon Releasing

- Spiritual Gifts

- Artists and Marriage

Archangel Jophiel

- Beautifying Thoughts

- Loving Feelings

- Home and Office

- Self-love

- Learning New Things

- Inspiration

- Environment

- Negative to Positive

- Beauty

- Helps Clean Out the Old

Archangel Raphael

- Safe Travels

- New Business Avenues

- Helps Children

- Memory

- Knowledge and Healing

- Clears Away Fear and Stress

- Emotional Healing

- Helps to Find the Right Healer

Archangel Jeremiel

- Helps Those Who are Crossing Over

- Take Stock of Life

- Mentor

Jesus

- Protection

- Healing

- Life Messages

- Emotional Healing

- Friendship

- Comforter

- Loves Children

- Spiritual Gifts

Mother Mary

- Nurtures and Guides

- Healing, Music, Truth

- Love

- Protector

- Queen of Angels

- Helps Troubled Souls

- Helps Connect us to the Divine

- Self-love

- Illumination

Emotional Problems

Anxiety: *Michael, Metatron, Chamuel, Zadkiel, Jophiel, Raphael, Jesus, Mother Mary*

Chaos: *Chamuel, Raguel, Jophiel, Raphael, Jesus*

Conflict with Others: *Metatron, Chamuel, Zadkiel, Raguel, Jesus, Mother Mary*

Confusion: *Michael, Uriel, Zadkiel, Raguel, Jophiel, Jesus, Mother Mary*

Emotional Blocks: *Uriel, Sandalphon, Zadkiel, Raphael, Jesus, Mother Mary*

Fear: *Michael, Raphael, Jesus, Mother Mary*

Inner Conflict: *Chamuel, Zadkiel, Jophiel, Raphael, Jesus*

Lack of Love: *Mother Mary, Jesus, Jophiel, Raphael, Jesus*

Loneliness: *Zadkiel, Jophiel, Raphael, Jesus, Mother Mary*

Low Motivation: *Chamuel, Zadkiel, Jophiel, Raphael, Jesus, Mother Mary*

Low Self-esteem: *Chamuel, Zadkiel, Raguel, Jophiel, Raphael, Jesus, Mother Mary*

Negative Thoughts: *Michael, Metatron, Jophiel, Raphael, Jesus*

Old Energy: *Michael, Metatron, Raphael, Jesus*

Past Memories: *Michael, Zadkiel, Raziel, Raphael, Jesus*

Past Vows: *Michael, Raziel, Jesus*

Self-worth: *Zadkiel, Raguel, Jophiel, Raphael, Jesus, Mother Mary*

Physical Needs

Belongings (protection): *Michael, Raphael, Jesus*

Clutter: *Jophiel*

Conception, Pregnancy: *Gabriel, Jesus*

Daily Needs: *Chamuel, Ariel, Sandalphon, Jesus*

Healing: *Raphael, Ariel, Jesus, Mother Mary*

Memory: *Zadkiel, Raphael*

Missing Items: *Chamuel*

Prosperity: *Chamuel, Ariel, Sandalphon, Zadkiel*

Traveling (protection): *Michael, Raphael, Jesus*

Career

Business Ideas: *Uriel, Raphael*

Children Work: *Metatron, Sandalphon*

Communication: *Gabriel, Jesus*

Courage: *Michael, Gabriel, Jesus*

Creative Artist: *Gabriel, Uriel, Sandalphon, Zadkiel, Haniel, Raphael*

Environmental Work: *Ariel*

Job: *Chamuel, Zadkiel, Raziel*

Life's Purpose: *Michael, Uriel, Raziel, Raphael, Jesus*

Traveling: *Michael, Raphael, Jesus*

Spirituality

Connection to Divine: *Jesus, Sandalphon, Mother Mary*

Connection to Non-physical Nature: *Ariel*

Higher Wisdom: *Metatron, Uriel, Raziel, Raphael, Jesus, Mother Mary*

Life's Purpose: *Michael, Raziel, Jesus, Mother Mary*

Prayers: *Sandalphon, Jesus*

Protection from Low Energy: *Michael, Jesus*

Spiritual Gifts: *Metatron, Sandalphon, Raziel, Haniel, Jesus, Mother Mary*

Spiritual Practices: *Metatron, Raziel*

Support Spiritually: *Sandalphon, Raziel, Jesus*

Family

Children: *Gabriel, Metatron, Zadkiel, Jesus, Mother Mary*

Child's Gender: *Sandalphon*

Conception: *Gabriel, Jesus, Mother Mary*

Friendships: *Jesus, Raguel*

Marriage: *Raguel, Haniel*

Pregnancy: *Gabriel, Jesus, Mother Mary*

Relationships: *Metatron, Raguel, Jesus*

Unborn Children: *Gabriel, Sandalphon*

Death

Crossing Over: *Metatron, Jeremiel*

Nature

Connection to Nature: *Ariel, Jophiel*

Environmental Job: *Ariel, Jophiel*

Healing Animals: *Raphael, Ariel*

Safety in Nature: *Ariel*

Conclusion

This spiritual tool is to help you learn to work with the archangels, Jesus, and Mother Mary. If you feel drawn to a certain one and not another, that is perfectly fine. I believe they are all available to help assist us, but just like we have certain friends we 'click with' better, I feel it's the same way with our spiritual team. I hope you enjoyed this book, and I look forward to hearing your own personal stories about your experiences with the archangels.

Thank you for reading: *How to Work with Archangels.*

Memo: All photos are public domain. Some of the pictures don't match the specific angel.

Made in the USA
Coppell, TX
04 January 2021

47561083R00069